TABLE OF CONTENTS

DISCLAIMER AND TERMS OF USE AGREEMENT:

(Please Read This Before Using This Book)

This information is for educational and informational purposes only. The content is not intended to be a substitute for any professional advice, diagnosis, or treatment.

The authors and publisher of this book and the accompanying materials have used their best efforts in preparing this book.

The authors and publisher make no representation or warranties with respect to the accuracy, applicability, fitness, or completeness of the contents of this book. The information contained in this book is strictly for educational purposes. Therefore, if you wish to apply ideas contained in this book, you are taking full responsibility for your actions.

The authors and publisher disclaim any warranties (express or implied), merchantability, or fitness for any particular purpose. The author and publisher shall in no event be held liable to any party for any direct, indirect, punitive, special, incidental or other consequential damages arising directly or indirectly from any use of this material, which is provided "as is", and without warranties. As always, the advice of a competent legal, tax, accounting, medical or other professional should be sought where applicable.

The authors and publisher do not warrant the performance, effectiveness or applicability of any sites listed or linked to in this book. All links are for information purposes only and are not warranted for content, accuracy or any other implied or explicit purpose. No part of this may be copied, or changed in any format, or used in any way other than what is outlined within this course under any circumstances. Violators will be prosecuted.

BlueprintCashPro

Listen carefully please.

If you copy exactly what I reveal in here, I know as a fact you will start seeing some fast revenue come in. It's simple and super lucrative once you see what I do.

This method is something that I've been using to generate a fulltime income online (yes, more than enough to literally retire for life) with minimal effort.

It's a formula that has worked time and time again to add income streams and give yourself as many "pay raises" as you'd like.

The most successful guy doing this formula is now making well into the millions PER MONTH off this one technique!!

Now, that's one of the more extreme cases but even if you barely put any effort in, you be easily make a six figure income on autopilot.

You don't need a product, website, or anything – just a few "copy and paste" methods promoting certain products.

As we know promoting the right way will make us a lot of money. A LOT!

So how do we do this?

How do we know how and what to promote?

Well, here's a little secret I've been using under the radar. I use the power of a hidden network called Payzeno at: http://www.payzeno.com

This little network is pure gold. It is the source for proven templates on how to promote something so that it converts for you.

The merchants or product owners literally give you a blueprint (or exact recipe) on how to promote the products profitably.

These blueprints reveal the exact traffic sources and what ads and methods to use. So all you literally do is copy their template on how to promote.

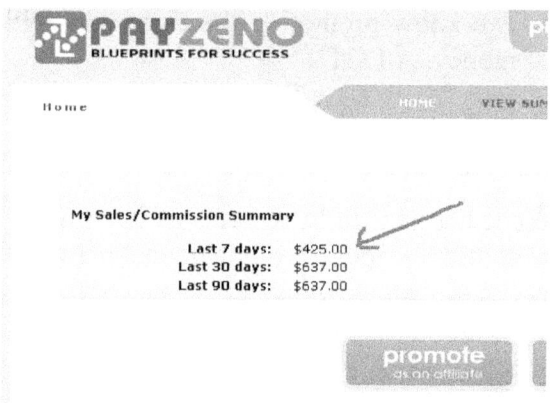

There is little margin of error when starting because you can just copy the template. It's proven to convert into commissions and bring you easy revenue since merchants have tested it.

I will be teaching you how to optimize it further so that your profits will skyrocket from making $50/day or $100/day to well over $1,000 a day using my strategies.

See this screenshot on the right, I had one Payzeno account that made this much in a few days and I literally forgot about it! Their templates work very well.

The STEP-BY-STEP Blueprint Cash Pro

So the basic steps to set up these income streams are as follows:

1. Sign up for a Payzeno Account here: http://www.payzeno.com/users/add

Make sure you use a PayPal account (get one here http://www.paypal.com as you will be paid directly to your PayPal). You will get an affiliate link to use and get credited for sales you refer through it. So your goal is to get targeted traffic to this affiliate link. Usually, this can be hard. However, see next how Payzeno solves this issue for us. Choose 'Promote' when you log in.

2. Copy some of the blueprints to promote – here is one example as they show exactly what to do to start earning: http://www.payzeno.com/blueprints/view/19. You can also select from the Top 5 products at the current moment and use one of the blueprints: http://www.payzeno.com/products/promotetopfive. All you need to do is to copy how it's done. If the blueprint says advertise, then you can bet that if you ran those ads like they show, it can convert well into earnings for you! Just follow the blueprint.

Method #1 Pay per click for some fast profits

Use these exact keywords:

```
rid man boobs
reduce man boobs
lose chest fat
lose man boobs
chest fat
man tits
man boobs
man boobs exercise
eliminate man boobs
chest exercise
chest weight training
chest work out
cliff manchaster
cliff manchester
men breasts
man breasts
male breast reduction
man breast reduction
men breast reduction
pectoral fat
puffy nipples
chest fat
gynecomastia
gynexin
```

Use this exact ad for these keywords:

Rid Your Man Boobs?

Eliminate Chest Fat And

Man Boobs Fast & Easy!

www.RidManBoobsFast.com

3. Keep adding new blueprints to your portfolio and expand your profits. I've copied many of the blueprints in this network and it's pure gold after you keep the roll going. So here's a detailed example from one of their blueprints:

http://www.payzeno.com/blueprints/view/22

I've used this blueprint and earned quite a bit. Here is a screenshot on the right -> So what we will do is first open some advertising accounts at search engines like

http://adwords.google.com or

http://sem.smallbusiness.yahoo.com/searchenginemarketing/ or

http://advertising.microsoft.com/searchadvertising

Method #2 - forum signature posting

http://www.gynecomastia.org/smf/

Post around and use this signature:

Get rid of your man boobs in 24 hours guaranteed:
<a href="http://payzeno.com/a/youid/22">Click here</a>

Method #3 - do content-targeting for the Adsense on this forum

http://www.elitefitness.com/forum/gynecomastia/

Use this exact ad:

Shocking Man Boob Cure
Eliminate Chest Fat And
Man Boobs Fast & Easy!
www.RidManBoobsFast.com

We then start up campaigns using that exact advertisement and keywords that the blueprint provides. That's one of the methods in the blueprint. Also, here's a screenshot above of yet another method in the blueprint.

The method #2 here involves us to post on the forum

http://www.elitefitness.com/forum/gynecomastia/

I will go inside and use that signature within my profile edit. Then, I'll contribute to the forum areas there – this also brings targeted traffic to my affiliate link to make some easy commissions! If you do nothing else, using and copying those templates will get you paid a nice stream of online revenue. You are now officially making money online! Easy right?

Now, the next step is to really grow your revenue streams from these templates. How do we take it to the next level? The answer is expanding and optimizing.

EXPANDING
So let's take another blueprint that shows you to advertise on keywords like: Reverse phone search Reverse cell lookup Phone number directory Etc… http://www.payzeno.com/blueprints/view/30. You can easily increase your profits by adding new keywords that the merchant has not even given out. Think … what types of keywords are searched by people who want this product? One idea for this is to add in phone numbers as keywords! Just look up "popularly searched phone numbers", see what they are and add those as your keywords. That's one example of expansion. Another example is … say you know this product is targeting people who are doing reverse phone lookups. What other websites on the internet contain people who are after this? Detective websites for example! You can find those and start advertising on them. This will expand the traffic you bring to your affiliate link as well as earn you more commissions than even the blueprints themselves can.

OPTIMIZING

This is not really needed but you can really increase your income even further this way. Another advanced trick to really expand your profits is to cloak your affiliate link on your own domain: http://www.YourDomain.com=>http://payzeno.com/a/yourid/xx

This can easily increase your profits because you can even print this domain on business cards and hand them out. This will also drive traffic and buyers through your affiliate link. Let's say you were targeting people looking for the reverse phone search product. You can place your business card in the phone booths' yellow pages. This can drive traffic to your domain – which contains your affiliate link. Having your domain also decreases costs on pay per click for the search engines – did you know?

Optimizing is really just tweaking what the blueprints already show you and MILKING more profits from proven channels of traffic. So this is how my technique works. I found this network/marketplace that offers exact recipes on how to promote stuff. I then copy their marketing blueprints and set it on autopilot.

Take action right now, and copy exactly what I revealed to you here. It will be some fast revenue just via those blueprints. As the merchants improve their blueprints, just keep copying these and your own income will increase over time as well.

Expanding your profits to the NEXT level: Becoming a Merchant on Payzeno

Note: If you read no further, you will still do very well with the blueprints as described above. However, this next section is for people who really desire to add EVEN more income.

Now, copying the various blueprints of the merchants on Payzeno can be very lucrative and easy. You can make a lot of money through it, but to me – another level begins if you do BOTH affiliate marketing using the blueprints AND sell your own product on Payzeno.

Creating and then placing up your own product on Payzeno is a slight bit more work than just being an affiliate and copying the blueprints. But just stick with me; it's not as hard as you think ;) It is another powerful income stream with its own advantages, and actually very rewarding.

The beauty of it is that you can literally sell ANYTHING on here and get paid directly via your PayPal account. Then just test out a good converting blueprint (profitable for affiliates) and other affiliates will automatically help you!

So first thing is first .... What products can I create? The key to this is EASY once you get it.... Find a hot selling market. Contrary to what many people believe, it's better to sell something that is HOT at the moment (despite heavy competition – rather than some obscure market where there is little competition). Also, if you're using Payzeno to sell, competition will have little effect because a good, proven blueprint will take you above and beyond. I'll explain in a little bit here.

DO NOT WASTE TIME with small, obscure markets or products. So what are some hot selling markets?

How to lose weight

How to save money

How to make extra money

How to attract the opposite sex

How to trade stocks well

How to get a six pack bodybuilding

See these ideas? Pick one and do your own spin on it. Let's take the weight loss market. I can sell "Mr.

X's diet system" assuming I can authentically create something of real value here. As you can tell, I personally like information products, such as selling ebooks on Payzeno.

HINT: Here's one market that will do well in the near future I know – it's "how to make money on Payzeno".

Yes, I'll be releasing a great top of the line product here since I've had a lot of success being an affiliate with Payzeno's blueprints. The public blueprints are great income, but I still have some super secrets that raise it to astonishing income. You may want to consider this as well.

Next, how would you create this product; for example – ebooks? You can generally write them yourself and place them up on a website. You can also hire an expert to write them by going to sites like http://www.guru.com.

If you're looking to sell physical products, then you need to find a distributor and suppliers for this. As for your product website, make sure to present your product in a good light. Describe its benefits and how it will help the person. Don't be afraid to toot your horn about how well your product does for another. If you don't know how to set up a web page to effectively describe your product, then hire someone at http://www.guru.com called "copywriters". Finally, how do you create a blueprint for this product?

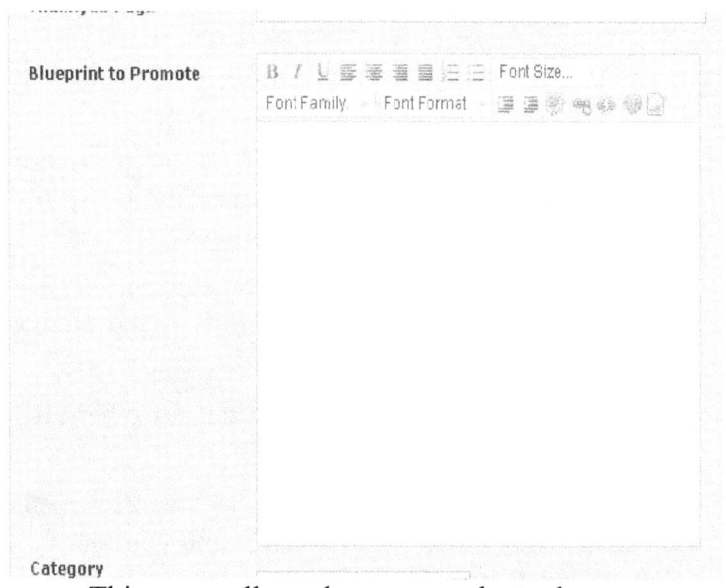

Blueprint to Promote

Category

This can really make your product a huge success – so pay attention here. This may be the toughest part BUT it's really not that hard. One of the easiest, surefire ways to create a blueprint is by going to:

https://adwords.google.com/select/KeywordToolExternal

Click on "Website content" and then enter your product website URL. This will give you the relevant keywords that people looking for your product may be searching for. Now, run an advertisement on the pay per click search engines. Wait for many clicks and see which keywords

CONVERT the best. See which keywords convert at a high rate.

These are the keywords to add to your blueprint for that product.

It's best to test very well first before giving it out – because other affiliates will trust you to test things before they try to promote your products.

This is built on your reputation as a merchant so only give out blueprints you have thoroughly tested and proven to convert into product sales.

When in doubt, keep testing and seeing which traffic sources convert well, before giving them on your blueprint.

Also give your exact ad out for other affiliates to use.

There, you now have one blueprint method that affiliates can take without effort and confidently convert well, ideally into profits fast!

Another way to add more methods for other affiliates to copy and profit – is to find forums related to your product.

Do a search on this.

For example, let's say you are selling a dog training book and kit. Look for popular DOG TRAINING FORUMS.

Then, start posting with a signature or advertise your product on this forum.

If this medium makes you sales and is profitable, THEN you can safely place it in your product blueprint for others to use too.

Never forget – TEST, TEST, and TEST until ideally you see those traffic sources are profitable for other affiliates.

Never stop IMPROVING your blueprint either and adding more proven methods.

The other affiliates will love you for this!

Now, you have your blueprint, your product, and the Payzeno marketplace will automatically help you like nothing else out there.

That's it!

Now, you have your own product and blueprint driving an additional layer of income for you day in and day out. Life gets very good at this point! Now, I've shown you two very powerful exact recipes to do with this hidden little marketplace. Copy this technique immediately and you will be thanking yourself. This, I can promise you.

*****

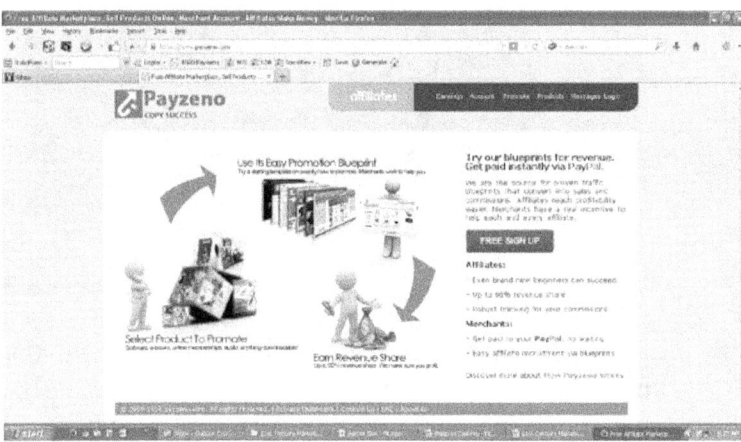

17

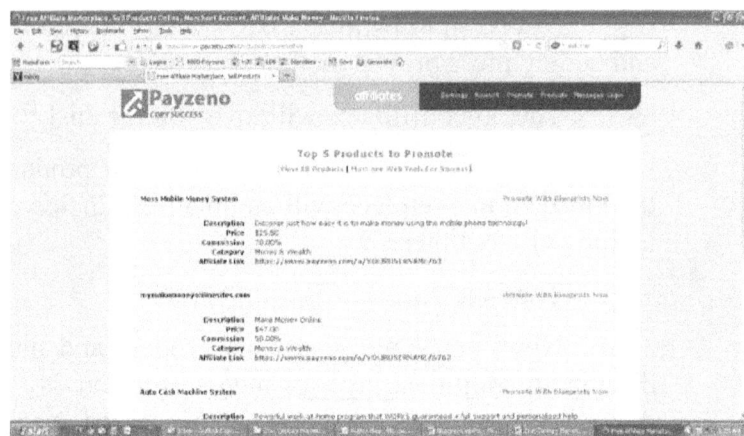

https://www.payzeno.com/products/promotetopfive

Also check this site out too…

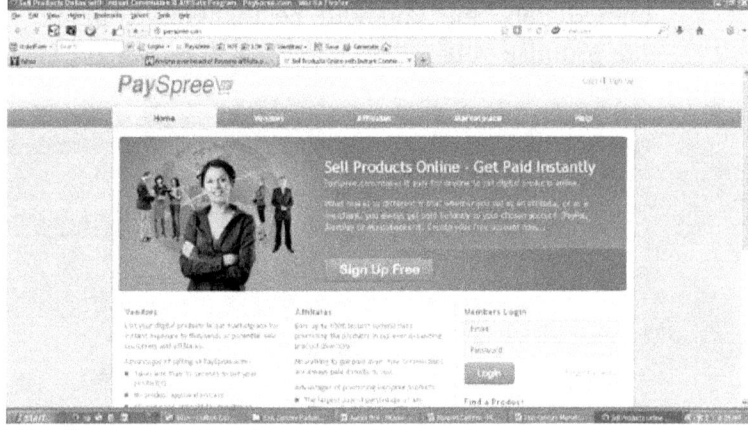

http://payspree.com/

The difference in these two sites is that Payzeno does not pay instant PayPal commissions for affiliates, only the merchants get paid instantly then they have to pay their affiliates monthly. PaySpree does pay instant affiliate commissions.

Feedback - Pay Zeno Description

18

Pay Zeno is an affiliate marketing network that provides people with a list of digital downloadable products to promote for commissions or "revenue share". Commission income can vary according to the merchant. This affiliate marketing network benefits merchant as well by attracting affiliates to promote their products, thus increasing their sales volumes.

Pay Zeno Detailed Overview

There are a few affiliate networks⍈ on the internet today; some that are well known and some that are not quite as well known. Though Pay Zeno is not as well known as some others, it is unique enough to get the attention of affiliate marketers once they come across it. Most affiliate networks list merchant products for their members to look over so that they can choose the products that they want to promote. Affiliate networks usually also provide some tools, resources and advice for effective marketing. This program does that, but it adds a twist.

When you sign up with Pay Zeno as an affiliate, you can search through the list for products to promote. With each product on the list you are given information such as who the merchant is, the link for their sales website, and how much commission they will pay to affiliates. When you find⍈ one that you're interested in, you can click on the link next to it in the list that says "promote with blueprints now". When you click on that link, you are taken to a page that gives you the merchant's blueprint for marketing the product. These blueprints, provided by the merchants themselves, can contain keywords for affiliates to use in their campaigns, exact ads or banners to use, and even information on affiliate links to put in forum posts. This can be very helpful for promotions.

Some merchants provide detailed marketing blueprints for affiliates, while others provide only a minimum amount of information.

It doesn't cost anything to join up with the Pay Zeno affiliate network. Affiliates are paid commissions through the network directly to their PayPal accounts. Only merchants pay fees to belong to the network.

Pay Zeno Reputation

There is not a lot of feedback on the Pay Zeno affiliate network. This is not surprising, as it is one of the newer networks. From what little information there is, it looks like the program does pay its affiliates, and the blueprint system is a good way to help anyone interested in promoting the products. The fact that there don't seem to be any negative comments about the service is a good sign also. It could be worth a try for people who are interested in affiliate marketing.

WWW.PAYZENO.COM

Visit www.payzeno.com

General Info

Stats & Details Whois IP Whois Collapse all blocks

Free Affiliate Marketplace, Sell Products Online, Merchant Account, Affiliates Make Money

Try free blueprints to start affiliate marketing products online and earn. Merchants can sell their product online easily and let us bring the traffic.

Keywords: marketplace, conversion, Payzeno, affiliate, marketing, affiliate marketplace, free marketplace to sell products, Payzeno, bagaimana blueprint payzeno

Daily visitors: 961

Daily pageviews: 4 807

Alexa Rank: 1040623

Created: 2009-06-07

Expires: 2014-06-07
Hosting company: Unified Layer
Registrar: GODADDY.COM, LLC
IPs: 198.57.197.75
DNS: ns1.payzeno.com
ns2.payzeno.com
Payzeno.com thumbnail
Stats & Details
Alexa.com
Traffic Rank: 1040623
Month Average Daily Reach: 0.00018
        +1300%
Month Average Daily Pageviews: 0.000009
        +1200%
Month Average Pageviews per user: 5   -0.6%
Alexa Search Traffic
Compare this site to:
Mywot.com - Reputation rating
Trustworthiness:
        60
Vendor reliability:
        60
Privacy:
        60
Yahoo.com
Backlinks to homepage: 2
Backlinks domain wide: 2 310
Compete.com
Visits: 9 554   +110.72%
Whois
Whois Server Version 2.0

Domain names in the .com and .net domains can now be registered with many different competing registrars. Go to http://www.internic.net for detailed information.

  Domain Name: PAYZENO.COM
  Registrar: GODADDY.COM, LLC
  Whois Server: whois.godaddy.com
  Referral URL: http://registrar.godaddy.com
  Name Server: NS1.PAYZENO.COM
  Name Server: NS2.PAYZENO.COM
  Status: clientDeleteProhibited
  Status: clientRenewProhibited
  Status: clientTransferProhibited
  Status: clientUpdateProhibited
  Updated Date: 08-jun-2013
  Creation Date: 07-jun-2009
  Expiration Date: 07-jun-2014

>>> Last update of whois database: Wed, 06 Nov 2013 00:45:53 UTC <<<

NOTICE: The expiration date displayed in this record is the date the registrar's sponsorship of the domain name registration in the registry is currently set to expire. This date does not necessarily reflect the expiration date of the domain name registrant's agreement with the sponsoring registrar. Users may consult the sponsoring registrar's Whois database to view the registrar's reported date of expiration for this registration.

TERMS OF USE: You are not authorized to access or query our Whois database through the use of electronic processes that are high-volume and automated except as reasonably necessary to register domain names or modify existing registrations; the Data in VeriSign Global Registry

Services' ("VeriSign") Whois database is provided by VeriSign for information purposes only, and to assist persons in obtaining information about or related to a domain name registration record. VeriSign does not guarantee its accuracy. By submitting a Whois query, you agree to abide by the following terms of use: You agree that you may use this Data only for lawful purposes and that under no circumstances will you use this Data to: (1) allow, enable, or otherwise support the transmission of mass unsolicited, commercial advertising or solicitations via e-mail, telephone, or facsimile; or (2) enable high volume, automated, electronic processes that apply to VeriSign (or its computer systems). The compilation, repackaging, dissemination or other use of this Data is expressly prohibited without the prior written consent of VeriSign. You agree not to use electronic processes that are automated and high-volume to access or query the Whois database except as reasonably necessary to register domain names or modify existing registrations. VeriSign reserves the right to restrict your access to the Whois database in its sole discretion to ensure operational stability. VeriSign may restrict or terminate your access to the

Whois database for failure to abide by these terms of use. VeriSign reserves the right to modify these terms at any time.

The Registry database contains ONLY .COM, .NET, .EDU domains and Registrars.

IP Whois

ARIN WHOIS data and services are subject to the Terms of Use

available at: https://www.arin.net/whois_tou.html

The following results may also be obtained via:

#http://whois.arin.net/rest/nets;q=198.57.197.75?showDe
tails=true&showARIN=false&ext=netref2
NetRange: 198.57.128.0 - 198.57.255.255
CIDR: 198.57.128.0/17
OriginAS: AS46606
NetName: UNIFIEDLAYER-NETWORK-12
NetHandle: NET-198-57-128-0-1
Parent: NET-198-0-0-0-0
NetType: Direct Allocation
RegDate: 2012-07-27
Updated: 2012-11-14
Ref: http://whois.arin.net/rest/net/NET-198-57-
128-0-1
OrgName: Unified Layer
OrgId: BLUEH-2
Address: 1958 South 950 East
City: Provo
StateProv: UT
PostalCode: 84606
Country: US
RegDate: 2006-08-08
Updated: 2012-11-26
Ref: http://whois.arin.net/rest/org/BLUEH-2
ReferralServer: rwhois://rwhois.unifiedlayer.com:4321
OrgNOCHandle: NETWO5508-ARIN
OrgNOCName: Network Operations
OrgNOCPhone: +1-888-401-4678
OrgNOCEmail: netops@unifiedlayer.com
OrgNOCRef:
http://whois.arin.net/rest/poc/NETWO5508-ARIN
OrgTechHandle: NETWO5508-ARIN
OrgTechName: Network Operations
OrgTechPhone: +1-888-401-4678

OrgTechEmail: netops@unifiedlayer.com
OrgTechRef:
http://whois.arin.net/rest/poc/NETWO5508-ARIN
OrgAbuseHandle: ABUSE3581-ARIN
OrgAbuseName: Abuse Department
OrgAbusePhone: +1-888-401-4678
OrgAbuseEmail: abuse@unifiedlayer.com
OrgAbuseRef:
http://whois.arin.net/rest/poc/ABUSE3581-ARIN
ARIN WHOIS data and services are subject to the Terms of Use
available at: https://www.arin.net/whois_tou.html
%rwhois V-1.5:000080:00 rwhois.unifiedlayer.com (by Unified Layer, V-1.0.0)
network:Class-Name:network
network:ID: NETBLK-UL.198.57.197.75/32
network:Auth-Area: 198.57.197.75/32
network:Network-Name: UL-198.57.197.75/32
network:IP-Network: 198.57.197.75/32
network:Organization: websitewelcome.com
network:Tech-Contact: abuse@websitewelcome.com
network:Admin-Contact: abuse@websitewelcome.com
network:Abuse-Contact: abuse@websitewelcome.com
network:Created: 20130103
network:Updated: 20130103
network:Updated-By: abuse@websitewelcome.com
%ok
Found by
Make Account
Similar sites
elitemindsinc.com
Elite Minds Inc - Personal Development and Improvement

paydotcom.com
Sell Products Online, Sell Online, Affiliate Marketplace,
Sell Products Online With PayPal, Affiliate Marketing,
Merchant Accounts, Free Product Listing, Digital
Products, Affiliate Network, Promote P...
paydotcom.net
Sell Products Online, Sell Online, Affiliate Marketplace,
Sell Products Online With PayPal, Affiliate Marketing,
Merchant Accounts, Free Product Listing, Digital
Products, Affiliate Network, Promote P...
cbgraph.com
A Professional ClickBank Marketplace | CBGraph
peakprofits.com
An affiliate network offering performance based CPL,
CPA, CPS campaigns, featuring quick and reliable
customer support and state of the art reporting system.

I Have a Special Gift for My Readers

I appreciate my readers for without them I am just another author attempting to make a difference. If my book has made a favorable impression please leave me an honest review. Thank you in advance for you participation.

My readers and I have in common a passion for the written word as well as the desire to learn and grow from books.

My special offer to you is a massive ebook library that I have compiled over the years. It contains hundreds of fiction and non-fiction ebooks in Adobe Acrobat PDF format as well as the Greek classics and old literary classics too.

In fact, this library is so massive to completely download the entire library will require over 5 GBs open on your desktop.

Use the link below and scan all of the ebooks in the library. You can select the ebooks you want individually or download the entire library.

The link below does not expire after a given time period so you are free to return for more books rather than clog your desktop. And feel free to give the link to your friends who enjoy reading too.

I thank you for reading my book and hope if you are pleased that you will leave me an honest review so that I can improve my work and or write books that appeal to your interests.

Okay, here is the link…

http://tinyurl.com/special-readers-promo

PS: If you wish to reach me personally for any reason you may simply write to mailto:support@epubwealth.com.

I answer all of my emails so rest assured I will respond.

Meet the Author

Dr. Leland Benton is Director of Applied Web Info, a holding company for ePubWealth.com, a leading ePublisher company based in Utah. With over 21,000 resellers in over 22-countries, ePubWealth.com is a leader in ePublishing, book promotion, and ebook marketing.

As the creator and author of "The ePubWealth Program," Leland teaches up-and-coming authors the ins-and-outs of today's ePublishing world. He has assisted hundreds of authors make it big in the ePublishing world.

Leland also created a series of external book promotion programs and teaches authors how to promote their books using external marketing sources.

Leland is also the Managing Director of Applied Mind Sciences, the company's mind research unit and Chief Forensics Investigator for the company's ForensicsNation unit. He is active in privacy rights through the company's PrivacyNations unit and is an expert in survival planning and disaster relief through the company's SurvivalNations unit.

Leland resides in Southern Utah.

Visit some of his websites

http://www.AddMeInNow.com
http://www.AppliedMindSciences.com
http://www.BookbuilderPLUS.com
http://www.BookJumping.com
http://www.EmailNations.com
http://www.EmbarrassingProblemsFix.com
http://www.ePubWealth.com
http://www.ForensicsNation.com
http://www.ForensicsNationStore.com
http://www.FreebiesNation.com
http://www.HealthFitnessWellnessNation.com
http://www.Neternatives.com
http://www.PrivacyNations.com
http://www.RetireWithoutMoney.org
http://www.SurvivalNations.com
http://www.TheBentonKitchen.com
http://www.Theolegions.org
http://www.VideoBookbuilder.com